From Spatial Development to Detail

Notatio

Emmanuel Rey

From Spatial Development to Detail

Quart Publishers Lucerne

Emmanuel Rey
From Spatial Development to Detail
Volume 4 of the Series Notatio

Author: Emmanuel Rey
English translation: Benjamin Liebelt, Berlin
Plans and illustrations: Bauart
Photos: Yves André, Vaumarcus NE S. 23, 26, 31, 34, 67, 70;
Thomas Jantscher, Colombier NE S. 41, 58/59, 62;
Ruedi Walti, Basel S. 44
Graphic design: Quart Verlag, Antonia Wirz
Lithos: Printeria, Luzern
Printing and binding: DZA Druckerei zu Altenburg GmbH

Original edition 2014: French (ISBN 978-3-03761-091-6)
German edition 2014 (ISBN 978-3-03761-090-9)

Quart Verlag GmbH
Denkmalstrasse 2, CH-6006 Luzern
Telefon +41 41 420 20 82, E-Mail books@quart.ch
www.quart.ch

prohelvetia

Content

This publication is based on a lecture held by Emmanuel Rey on June 5, 2012 at the Centre culturel suisse in Paris.

The Centre culturel suisse is dedicated to raising awareness of contemporary, cosmopolitan Swiss cultural achievements in France, supporting the external profile of Swiss artists and strengthening connections between the French and Swiss art scenes. The ambitious programme of the Centre culturel suisse focuses on contemporary Swiss artworks and reflects their diversity. In doing so, it is not limited to the exhibition of visual art, but also includes dance, music, theatre, literature, film and architecture in its programme. Among the architects recently invited to present their visions and projects are Andrea Deplazes, Christ & Gantenbein, Gigon & Guyer, Gion A. Caminada, Herzog & de Meuron, Luigi Snozzi and Peter Zumthor.

centre culturel **suisse** • paris

Foreword
Jean-Paul Felley & Olivier Kaeser

Lectures on architecture are a key programme element of the Centre culturel suisse in Paris. The evening events that have been held periodically since 2009 attract large audiences; some events are presented in cooperation with the Centre Pompidou. Furthermore, the Architecture Department of the CCS library is particularly attractive and well stocked. Swiss architecture is attracting growing attention in France and around the world, and this is not simply due to great, Pritzker Prize-winning stars.

In 2012, several lectures by architects focused on the theme of ecology and sustainability, an issue that today's architecture cannot ignore. The small series presented three especially characteristic positions on this theme: one developed by Andrea Desplazes and his students at the ETH Zurich for the new high-tech lodge on Monte Rosa, one by Gion A. Caminada with his exemplary conversion and renovation of locally typical buildings in the Grisons village of Vrin, and finally one by the office Bauart, with its superb redesign of the station quarter in Neuchâtel. The result was a veritable tour of Switzerland that led from urban Central Switzerland over the peaks of the Alps and on to small mountainous villages.

Each time we pass Neuchâtel on trips to Switzerland, we take a look at the tower of the Federal Statistics Office built by Bauart. It recalls memories of a lecture held by Emmanuel Rey at our institute. He not only runs the renowned office with his partners, but has also been teaching Sustainable Architecture at the EPFL Lausanne since 2010. The tower is only the most prominent part of the Ecoparc quarter, an impressive ensemble of buildings developed in this Tuscan-style city.

In addition to all the major projects designed by Bauart, including the office tower, the school, the research centre and the shopping centre, we are also impressed by the small, 64 m² timber house consisting of two modules placed on top of each other, which were completely produced in the workshop and can be erected in a single day. Smallhouse is an experimental, poetic project; it was developed in 2000 and is experiencing a continuation today in urban residential buildings, where apartments can be combined according to the requirements of the users.

The word "Bauart" consists of "Bau" ("building") and "art", while alluding to the fact that it is possible to build according to the rules of art and take form and function into account. The name also combines the two languages of German and French, which give Switzerland its special character and cultural differences – a combination of Germanic discipline and Latin flexibility. The Bauart office, which is based on both sides of this so-called "Rösti Barrier", in Neuchâtel, Bern and Zurich, seems to have found a magic formula with which Swiss Architecture gains a radiance reaching far beyond its national boundaries.

Paris, autumn 2014

The Architectural Project in View of Global Challenges

Today, sustainable development plays an essential role in most fields of activities as a concept with a wide range of facets: on the level of theoretical reflections and in terms of political principles and envisaged targets. Its concrete implementation however is still in an experimental phase and raises numerous questions.[1] Sustainability is a regulatory idea and therefore a term, "that can never be precisely defined, but to which must constantly be referred."[2] The conceptual aim of "sustainable development" therefore requires an open, reflective approach that is grasped as an iterative process with development potential.[3] The developed environment has a decisive place in such considerations. In its quality as a space for living, producing

[1] Emmanuel Rey: Le développement durable appliqué à l'environnement construit. In: Régénération des friches urbaines et développement durable. Vers une évaluation intégrée à la dynamique du projet. Louvain-la-Neuve: Presses universitaires de Louvain 2012. p. 42–49

[2] Pierre-Alain Rumley: Constructions à courte durée de vie et aménagement du territoire national. In: Tracés, 22/2003. p. 28–30

[3] Alain Thierstein/Stéphane Decoutère: Nouvelle gestion publique et développement durable: une jonction impossible? In: Antonio Da Cunha et al.: Développement durable et aménagement du territoire. Lausanne: PPUR 2003. p. 141–164

and consuming, it raises many ecological, socio-cultural and economic questions. The way one changes the developed environment, approaches it and uses it, can significantly influence the global balance on which the term sustainability is based. This opens up such a broad field of themes that direct translation to the level of operative action is by no means easy. Bruno Peuportier for instance concluded in this respect that a client who demands a building for his programme that fulfils today's requirements without neglecting the needs of future generations certainly does not make the Building Manager's task any easier.[4] The aim of sustainability is indeed comprehensive in order to be translated into a concrete procedure.

According to the general definitions of the concept, one could perhaps define a sustainability that relates to the developed environment as the search for a balance between its ecological, socio-cultural and economic aspects. That means keeping sight of a whole number of underlying aims and especially harmonising them all. Sustainability with respect to the environment (or physical sustainability) implies ecological improvement in the framework of physical conditions and the ideal use of resources. Socio-cultural sustainability addresses the balance between social conditions and enhancing parameters that contribute to structuring

[4] Bruno Peuportier: Eco-conception des bâtiments. Bâtir en préservant l'environnement. Paris: Presses de l'Ecole des Mines 2003

12

the identity of society. Economic sustainability relates to the efficiency of processes and a balanced dynamism between the different processes.

The real challenge for those participating in the transformation of the developed environment lies in conceiving measures by which the underlying targets can be achieved – favouring those that facilitate the simultaneous occurrence of positive effects in other areas of sustainability. From a conceptual perspective, a regional planning, urban development or architectural project can be regarded as sustainable if it contributes to achieving those aims in as holistic – or at least as comprehensive – a way as possible. If the projects in question are unable to contribute to all targets simultaneously, they must at least strive to support the three dimensions inherent in sustainability. This operative perspective focuses on implementing projects that are technically appropriate and ecologically and economically viable, as well as creating added value on a sociocultural level. The step from a target to concrete action requires an extension of focus to include the decision-making processes involved in every project. Such a further development is comparable to a comprehensive study, an enhancement to include parameters that are usually taken into account in the field of building (costs, timetables, function), going beyond the purely environmentally-related requirements.

In accordance with the scale and spatial characteristics of the project in question, these optimised processes can assume various forms, which often develop out of a combination of the three following operative dimensions: a holistic approach (integrating all characteristics of the project), an interdisciplinary, participatory approach (integrating many participants and competencies) and an evaluating approach (proactive visualisation of the expected effect). It should be noted that the necessity of an evaluating approach is an integral element of the concept of sustainable development. Agenda 21 is explicitly committed to using "information as an aid to decision-making".[5]

Applying the concept of sustainability to architecture leads one to question the approaches of the economic boom years, which still influence many practical aspects of construction and building management today. Beyond aesthetic questions, a project today is confronted by a wide range of questions that reach beyond architecture in the strict sense.

Diverse approaches – both in a qualitative and a quantitative sense – have proven to be essential to grasp the complexity that such developments involve. The structure of this book, which focuses on six major questions, reflects the extent and diversity of the problems faced by today's architectural projects. Each of these fields of problems is initially presented on a theoretical level and then explained using the example of a concrete project by Bauart. Without claiming to be comprehensive, this approach can thereby

[5] United Nations: Agenda 21: The United Nations programme of action from Rio. New York: UN Publications 1993

present the office's research procedure – with its both re-
sourceful and pragmatic character. Secondly, it can demon-
strate how spatial, typological, structural and technical alternatives emerge that, each in its own scale, become part
of a development that strives towards sustainability for
the built environment.[6]

[6] Willi Frei/Emmanuel Rey: Du territoire au détail constructif. In: Thierry
Mandoul et al.: Climats. Les conférences de Malaquais. Paris: Ecole nationale supérieure d'architecture de Paris - Malaquais 2012. p. 441– 473

Urban Densification

Questioning urban sprawling

Urban densification plays an important role where theoretical reflection and concrete experimentation meet. In the context of the post-industrial European city, the decay of conurbations into a sprawl of undefined neighbouring peripheral areas has a wide range of negative consequences – in ecological, socio-cultural and economic terms.[7]

The urban sprawl is primarily an unreasonable use of land and therefore not only should be regarded as a waste of that resource, but also has a negative effect on the landscape's appearance. The spatial separation of urban functions also leads to an increase in environmental burdens mainly due to the greater distances travelled and the increased importance of individual transport. Since the areas for living, working, shopping and leisure continue to be separated, many residents are heavily dependent on their cars, leading to increased energy consumption, as well as

[7] Emmanuel Rey: Les territoires de la densité. In: Emmanuel Rey (ed.): Green Density. Lausanne: Presses polytechniques et universitaires romandes 2013. p. 25–36

congested streets and air pollution in the cities.[8] According to a Swiss study, this also has economic consequences.[9] Despite all efforts to extend the sewage, transport and supply networks, some peripheral zones are more poorly supplied than others, which creates socio-economic disparities. From a sociological perspective, a diverse settlement development therefore contradicts the aim of a long-term balance.[10]

In view of such results, there has been consensus for around a decade that urban densification should be encouraged. Urban development strategy poses complex challenges to architects with respect to spatial qualities: Deserted locations must be newly occupied; new, contemporary areas must be integrated in intermediary spaces in the existing structure; already urbanised areas must be transformed. That includes the rejuvenation of urban wastelands as one of the highest priorities. It enables a qualitative densification within the existing developed structure and the multi-dimensional revitalisation of specific districts and conurbations.[11]

[8] Peter Newman / Jeffrey Kenworthy: Sustainability and Cities. Overcoming Automobile Dependence. Washington: Island Press 1999
[9] ARE: Coûts des infrastructures. Bern: ARE 2000
[10] Marc Sauvez: La ville et l'enjeu du développement durable. Paris: La Documentation française 2001
[11] Emmanuel Rey: Des friches urbaines aux quartiers durables. In: Tracés, 12/2007. p. 13–15

Ecoparc: From a railway wasteland to a sustainable quarter
Although a whole series of such projects have been undertaken in Europe for around a decade, many of them are only implicitly or superficially dedicated to the concept of sustainability. The establishment of a sustainable quarter on a stretch of fallow railway land in Neuchâtel can be regarded as a pioneering measure in that respect.[12] As a result of the competition to build the Federal Statistics Office and densify the neighbouring area, which Bauart won in 1990, a new, densely developed quarter that is well connected to the public transport system was to be created. Old buildings were to be converted into loft apartments and new residential, administrative, school and multifunctional buildings were planned.[13]

Morphologically, the new urban pole is characterised by integrated elements that explicitly stage the location's original period: the end of the 19th century, when the old Crêt-Taconnet hill was levelled for the railway line. Based on the resulting double-geometry – straight along the railway tracks and curved on the side of Lake Neuchâtel – a dialogue has unfolded between the elongated buildings along the railway line, the curved developments along the slope and the punctiform buildings lower down. The concept enhances the new quarter by highlighting the constitutive characteristics of the location, since it creates an

[12] Cécile Guiochon: Une greffe réussie au cœur de la ville. In: Systèmes solaires, 194/2009. p. 50–57
[13] Markus Jakob: Quartier Ecoparc Bauart #1. Basel/Berlin/Boston: Birkhäuser 2004

undeveloped open space at its core as a symbol of its new urban nature.[14]

In addition to aspects strictly committed to density, mixture and mobility, the project also integrates numerous facets of sustainability. With respect to scale and duration, the Ecoparc project represents a concrete sustainability experiment within the perimeter of a quarter. The complexity of the task requires a certain degree of inventiveness, not only on the levels of spatial development and expressive design, but also equally in terms of various processes developed to integrate all participants into its concretisation and operative supervision.[15] The Ecoparc project can especially be seen as a test run for two systems to evaluate sustainability on the level of quarters: SIPRIUS[16] and Quartiers durables by Smeo.[17] A series of sustainability criteria was defined for them.

The immediate vicinity of the station and the optimisation of parking spaces facilitated the use of public transport and acceptable forms of mobility (distances covered on

[14] Bruno Marchand: L'esprit de la ville. In: Quartier Ecoparc Bauart #2. Bâle/Berlin/Boston: Birkhäuser 2009. p. 21–37

[15] Malika Wyss et al.: De l'utopie au faire. Neuchâtel: Alphil 2010

[16] Emmanuel Rey: Application-test. In: Régénération des friches urbaines et développement durable. Vers une évaluation intégrée à la dynamique du projet. Louvain-la-Neuve: Presses universitaires de Louvain 2012. p. 149–185

[17] Emmanuel Rey: Quartiers durables. Défis et opportunités pour le développement urbain. Berne: Office fédéral du développement territorial ARE / Office fédéral de l'énergie OFEN 2011

foot or by bicycle). Numerous measures to the buildings themselves also limit the consumption of heat and electric power, for instance by integrating bioclimatic principles in the conception of buildings and using local resources. That is combined with an increased use of renewable energies: solar collectors, wood chip heating and geothermal probes. The total consumption of a household in the Ecoparc quarter in terms of the primary energy used for the building, the infrastructure and mobility is 50 % of the consumption of a household in a normal urban peripheral area.[18]

A high quality of life is also one of the central socio-cultural aims of the project. This is manifested in the high level of comfort in the apartments and the special focus on the design of the exterior spaces. Typologically, the majority are loggias that allow comprehensive privacy. Access to the public space at the centre of the quarter, which is exclusively for pedestrians, and the proximity to the public facilities equally contribute to the quarter's quality of life. The striving for typological diversity, which is particularly expressed in the variety of sizes and types of apartments, encourages the cross-generational mixture of residents.

Ecological aspects are central during the stages of operative implementation. In this case, the strategy involves several functional synergies, for instance pooling two schools

---

[18] Emmanuel Rey et al.: The influence of centrality on the global energy consumption in Swiss neighborhoods. In: Energy and Buildings, 60/2013. p. 75–82

in one building, creating a space-saving of almost 20 % compared to the initial programme for those rooms (concept of shared use of space).[19] On another level the new quarter contributes to enhancing the economic potential of the region. That is emphasised by the high population density, which underlines its intended role as a strategic pole. It consists of around 400 residents and employees per hectare, which is four times higher than the average in the city of Neuchâtel.[20]

[19] Werner Huber: Zahlen, Noten und Krawatten. In: Hochparterre, 11/2009. p. 56–59
[20] Emmanuel Rey: Integration of energy issues into the design process of sustainable neighborhoods. In: Proceedings of PLEA 2006. Geneva 2006. p. 679–682

Fig. 1

Ecoparc Quarter, Neuchâtel

Competition 1990/Construction period
(in stages) 1994–2017
Clients: Swiss Confederation (FSO),
Canton of Neuchâtel (Campus Arc 1),
CFF Immobilier (TransEurope), Bauart and
private clients (lofts), Helvetia (new rented
apartments), City of Neuchâtel (Passerelle du
Millénaire)
Architect: Bauart/W. Frei, R. Graf, S. Graf,
P. C. Jakob, E. Rey, Y. Ringeisen, M. Ryter
Collaboration: F. Agustoni, P. Benoit,
F. Brand, P. Brander, P. Brunner, Ch. Cottet,
G. Detruche, V. De Felice, G. De Pace,
S. d e Palézieux, L. Di Prinzio, A. Erard,
R. Fiechter, S. Fries, R. Gogniat, E. Guillaume,
G. Guth, U. Habermalz, F. Imthon-Zweifel,
M. Jansen-Alcayde, Y. Jolliet, M. Kull-Porchet,
Th. Lehmann, L. Marmy, F. Mani, J. Morais
Caldas, R. Moser, N. Mumenthaler, T. Parella,
P. Remund, L. Ruchet, N. Schneider,
R. Schori, R. Sulzer, M. Ulmer, A. Wavre,
P. Willich, A. Wimmer, V. Wörner, C. Zbinden

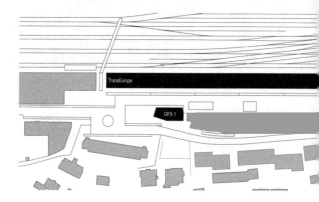

Fig. 2

Fig. 1: Aerial view
Fig. 2: Section
Fig. 3: Site plan
Fig. 4: Housing

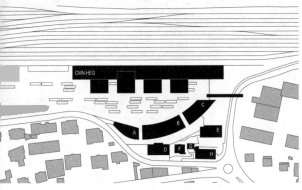

Fig. 3

Fig. 4

Transforming Existing Structures

Study on the ideal scale of measures
One thing will be fundamentally different in the coming decades compared to the past: Existing structures will become considerably more important. According to a report by the European Union, the city of the future can today be considered as almost 80 % developed.[21] Sustainability strategies must pursue a development logic based on given urban situations. These should be "reconceived" depending both on existing qualities and new perspectives.
In that sense, it is essential to take the important existing buildings into account. A study of residential buildings in Switzerland in 2000 showed that 48.6 % were built before 1960 and 39.3 % were built between 1961 and 1990.[22] If one assumes renovation cycles of 25 to 40 years, a growing proportion of existing buildings is ready for conversion.

---

[21] François Ascher et al.: European city visions: defining research needs (Workshop Report). Brussels, February 2001
[22] Michel Kornmann: La durée de vie des bâtiments en Suisse. 4ème Symposium sur les Energies Renouvelables et l'Environnement dans le bâtiment. Yverdon-les-Bains, November 2009

Architects must address a large number of possible scenarios when carrying out measures on existing buildings, from simple renovation to complete demolition, and subsequent new construction. In view of the latest studies on the field, one must accept that there is no clear answer either on an economic or ecological level as to what scope the relevant planned measures should have. Thus the decisions cannot be considered as implementing fixed recipes, but are instead the consequence of developing tailored approaches that are adapted to the specifics of each case.

In view of that fact, it is necessary to integrate a large number of factors – both economic and ecological – into the development of a project in order to prevent easily transferable quantitative criteria being over-weighted compared to equally important qualitative criteria that are however more difficult to determine. In particular, during the process of comparative evaluation, one must not forget the cultural value, especially when dealing with a historically interesting building, without it necessarily requiring the status of a monument.

Between a nostalgic stance that wishes to preserve everything and a desire for a *tabula rasa* that ignores the memory of a location, there are strategies for measures to existing buildings that are committed to the creative search for congruence between the developed frame and the changing functions accommodated within it. Such strategies can take into account contrasting aspects such as urban development, the architectural context, economic profitability, reduced energy consumption and more comfortable residential living. In that sense, the overall quality of the project is more strongly bound to the ideal coordination between the different parameters than to the quantitative improvement of individual fields.

Conversion of the old Cadolles Hospital

The conversion of the old Cadolles Hospital in Neuchâtel to create a new residential quarter is dedicated to such a process. Based on a masterplan for the entire estate, the building tasks consist of converting a number of existing buildings into single-storey privately owned apartments, while demolishing other buildings and developing new ones as freely rented and council housing.[23]

For the southern section of the estate that was created in 1914, which forms the central ensemble of the original hospital complex, the project plans around 30 new apartments that are accommodated in the main building, the old entrance lodge and a new section with a contemporary design, which replaces the old pavilion that is not retained.[24]

Initially, the extensions to the preserved buildings, which had been added during the course of the last century, were removed in order to regain the original volumetrics of the

[23] Stéphane Thiébaud: Les Cadolles à Neuchâtel: mise en concurrence d'investisseurs et d'architectes au service du projet urbain. In: Collage, 4/2008. p. 17–21
[24] Emilie Veillon: Renaissance contemporaine d'un bâtiment chargé d'histoire sur les hauts de la ville. In: Batimag, 8-9/2011. p. 14–20

buildings. Then modifications to the interior organisation were carried out by removing partition walls that were added as part of earlier conversion work. This restored the coherence, clarity and simplicity of the original situation.

Most of the retained buildings are situated in the southern section of the estate. Attractive, well structured façades, high ceilings, large-scale exterior spaces, good alignment towards the sun, a privileged relationship to the park and a view of Lake Neuchâtel and the Alps are all characteristic, identity-strengthening elements of this part of the estate. The apartments' day-use rooms are accommodated there, whereby the structure and original organisation of the building is retained. The corridor of the old hospital, which is a key typological element of the original composition, establishes a relationship with the outside space here and there through large new openings.

An extension will be built to the north of the building. It mainly accommodates the bedrooms and functional rooms, as well as a central staircase that supplements the two preserved staircases at the ends of the building. The roof of the main building has been significantly changed by introducing four new continuous volumes in a lightweight timber construction. The measures create exceptional apartments with a fine view and enhances the building's roof with architectural elements in a contemporary language.

The reinterpretation of the existing substance has led to a great diversity of apartments and spaces with a high degree of living quality. The powerful expression of the contours was retained despite the energy-related renovation measures.

Finally, the estate contributes to creating new housing in a densely urban environment. The overall approach demonstrates the entire range of concepts that can enhance a conversion project.

Fig. 1

Conversion of the old Cadolles Hospital, Neuchâtel

Competition 2006 (in cooperation with Bernasconi EG)/Construction period: 2008–2010
Clients: Bauart, subsequently the buyers of the owner-occupied apartments (PPE)
Architect: Bauart/W. Frei, R. Graf, S. Graf, P. C. Jakob, E. Rey, Y. Ringeisen, M. Ryter
Collaboration: P. Benoit, R. Bourgeois-Demaurex, A. Bulani, L. Di Prinzio, D. Dorsaz, Ch. Elbe, L. de Rham, R. Schori, C. Soltermann, A. Wavre
Site engineer: Peter Brunner

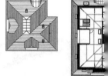

Fig. 1: Terrace of a loft apartment
Fig. 2: Site plan
Fig. 3: Elevation
Fig. 4: 4th floor plan
Fig. 5: 1st floor plan
Fig. 6: View from the public park to the southern façade

Fig. 2

32

Fig. 3

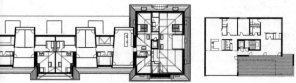

Fig. 4

Fig. 5

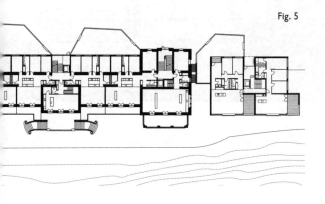

33

Fig. 6

Optimising the Consumption of Resources

Minimising the consumption of non-renewable resources
Currently, the developed environment only functions through the input of a considerable amount of external resources and produces masses of waste in the form of refuse and pollution. In view of the diverse consequences of this non-sustainable model, a number of optimisation strategies are required to achieve a new balance.[25] Minimising the consumption of non-renewable resources plays a key role in this respect. It involves improving effectiveness on the level of the individual building by reducing its energy requirements; secondly, with respect to land, energy, water and raw material requirements, recycled or renewable resources are preferable.

In strategies of this kind, energy – both heating energy and electricity – plays an important role. In fact more than 40 % of global energy consumption is in the building sector. Most European countries have set themselves ambitious targets to reduce energy consumption. In Switzerland, a country that is experiencing strong urbanisation, the total

---

[25] Emmanuel Rey: Vers la ville symbiotique? In: Actes de la 7ème édition du Forum Ecoparc: Vers la ville symbiotique? Valoriser les ressources cachées. Cahier spécial de la revue Tracés, November 2013. p. 3–5

energy consumption connected to buildings today is no less than half of overall energy requirements.[26] The model for the 2000 Watt society currently acts as a guideline for Swiss energy policy. Its aim is especially ambitious: The average consumption should be reduced by a factor of 3 in the long term.

Measures to reduce the energy requirements of a building are particularly based on taking bioclimatic principles into account even at the conceptual stage, as well as using sunlight, natural ventilation and passive air-conditioning. At the same time, the foreseeable end to the easy and cheap availability of fossil fuels, geopolitical tensions with respect to resources and the vulnerability of power grids all encourage the development of strategies that enable the secure provision of energy, in particular using local resources. That process not only requires a considerable reduction in consumption (economy), but also the comprehensive use of renewable energies (decentralised production). It requires the evaluation of available potential and decisions in favour of the most sustainable energy sources (e.g. solar power, biomass, geothermal energy, wind power), which are directly integrated into the building or, depending on the underlying conditions of the project, can be guaranteed through a connection to the long distance supply network.

[26] Emmanuel Rey et al.: Quartiers symbiotiques: augmenter le potentiel d'autonomie énergétique à l'échelle locale. In: Actes de la 7ème édition du Forum Ecoparc: Vers la ville symbiotique? Valoriser les ressources cachées. Cahier spécial de la revue Tracés, November 2013. p. 16–19

The Swiss Federal Statistical Office Tower

The 50-mtre high office tower of the Federal Statistical Office in Neuchâtel, which serves as an extension of the main building (for an additional 300 employees), is also a symbolic point of reference for an urban quarter that is experiencing comprehensive transformation.[27] The glass prism gives the station area a recognisable image. Its form, which is inspired by the context, and its glazed exterior façade appear to be opaque or reflective depending on the time of day.[28] With respect to the challenge represented by implementing a bioclimatic building with such a height, the chosen approach is an image of all efforts attempting to integrate the question of resources into architecture.

The project's core – resulting from intensive collaboration between the architects and engineers – is the implementation of a double-shelled façade. Its conceptualisation is complex, but it is simple to implement. Its closed position creates an external buffer zone that reduces the heating requirements in winter. During the non-heating period, its open position enables natural ventilation and protects

[27] Robert Walker: Ausrufezeichen am Bahnhof. In: Hochparterre, 3/2004. p. 46–48

[28] Judit Solt: Neuchâtel: Ein Prisma für die Stadt. In: Archithese, 3/2003. p. 56–59

interior openings and sun blinds from the wind. This system made it unnecessary to use a standard air-conditioning system due to the natural ventilation and passive air-conditioning.

However several research studies have discovered an increased risk of overheating in buildings with double-shelled façades.[29] Thus an especially good form of ventilation for the space between the two layers of the façade must be chosen and appropriate sun protection must be installed.[30] In this case, a series of dynamic simulations led to the decision in favour of a unilateral ventilation system with a separation between all floors in the buffer zone and staggered exterior openings to prevent pressure equalization effects.[31]

With respect to heating energy, the façade has excellent thermal performance. It allows it to benefit from internal heat gains and passive heat gains from the sunlight. The controlled ventilation limits heat losses by having openings generally closed and reducing the induced air to an absolute minimum using two-way ventilation. The heating requirements are covered by the installation of a heating

[29] André Faist et al.: La façade double-peau (EPFL – Research report). Lausanne 1998
[30] André Faist: Evolution dans la construction de façades: la façade double-peau. In: Fassade – Façade, 2/1999. p. 23–30
[31] Pierre Jaboyedoff et al.: Office fédéral de la statistique à Neuchâtel. Nouveau bâtiment, mise en service réelle, résultats énergétiques, conception de la nouvelle tour. In: Proceedings of CISBAT 2001. Lausanne 2001. p. 225–230

system in the neighbouring main building: It is powered by around 35 % solar power from a seasonal store (a 2,400 m^3 water reservoir combined with a 1,200 m^2 solar collector on the roof) and around 65 % by a gas heating system. The consumption achieved is a small indication of the heat energy consumption (final energy): It amounts to 25 kWh/m^2/year.

With respect to electrical energy, the façade openings and sun protection were dimensioned in a way to allow workplaces to benefit from the sunlight, while minimising unwanted heat transfer outside the heating period. In the summer, the automatic controls keep the windows open and the blinds lowered to reduce unwanted heat gains from the sun's radiation. The users can open and close the windows themselves as they wish and change the position of the blinds. They have however been made aware that it is in their interests to open the windows on the inner façade since the exterior temperature, especially at night (when it cools down) is lower than the interior temperature.

Due to the thermal mass of the building, the interior temperature is controlled passively and guarantees sufficient levels of comfort despite minimal electricity consumption. On especially hot days, two secondary systems are connected to the mechanical ventilation system (that is designed for wintry conditions): an adiabatic cooling system and a standard, powerful air-conditioning system. The two systems are automatically activated in the few hours in the year when they are essential. Special care was taken in choosing energy-efficient lighting and office machines. The success of combining such different strategies can be seen in the electricity consumption (final energy) measured after the building went into service, namely 31 kWh/m²/year.[32] Based on an analysis of the life cycle, building materials with a good environmental balance sheet and a high recycling factor were preferred, such as powder-coated steel for the façade, rather than aluminium. Such measures were reflected overall by the building's Minergie-Eco certification.

[32] Emmanuel Rey / Dario Aiulfi: Double-skin façade as a contribution to sustainable architecture: the Federal Office of Statistics tower in Neuchâtel (Switzerland). In: Proceedings of CISBAT 2005. Lausanne 2005. p. 83–88

Fig. 1

FSO Tower, Neuchâtel

Competition 1990 / Construction period
2000–2004
Client: Swiss Confederation
Architect: Bauart / W. Frei, R. Graf, S. Graf,
P. C. Jakob, E. Rey, Y. Ringeisen, M. Ryter
Collaboration: P. Brander, R. Moser,
P. Remund
Site engineer: Peter Brunner

Fig. 1: Double-layered façade
Fig. 2: Site plan
Fig. 3: Section
Fig. 4: 5th floor plan
Fig. 5: Insertion into the city

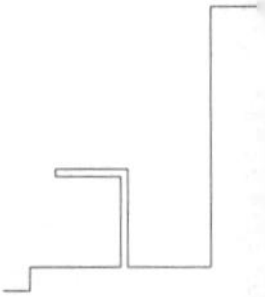

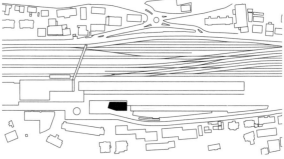

Fig. 2

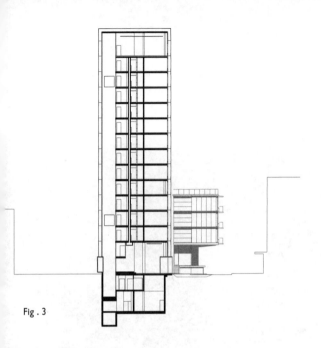

Fig . 3

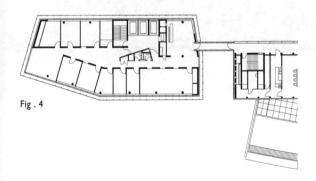

Fig . 4

Fig. 5

Anticipating Social Developments

Demographic change

Incorporating sustainability into an architectural project requires taking a long-term perspective. It is particularly important to take requirements into account that will emerge in the coming decades as a result of demographic and social changes. In most European countries in recent decades, there has been a strong transformation in the family structure and a tendency towards older average ages.

These developments have a comprehensive effect on the future composition of households. According to statistical forecasts, the proportion of Swiss households with more than two persons by the year 2030 will only be 24 %. The majority of people will live in single-person (41 %) or two-person (35 %) households.[33] This development in requirements must be anticipated by developing new housing types: Until now they have still often referred to a traditional family consisting of a married couple with two children.

[33] OFS: Forum Ecoparc 2009. Quelques données de l'Office fédéral de la statistique. Neuchâtel: Actualités OFS, January 2009. p. 4

The results undermine the trend towards the model of a single family home in a suburban location, as experienced for several decades. Until now, migration away from suburbs by the first generation of the residents has been largely compensated by new families moving into them, since they also prefer that form of living. In view of the current demographic change, this automatic renewal of the suburban population could fall away in the near future.

Several focuses of action must be undertaken in parallel to minimise this risk and integrate suburban living space as far as possible into strategies for a sustainable regional development. The first focus addresses regional planning and consists of adapting the allocated development zones. They are currently often oversized and poorly located with respect to actual demographic requirements.[34] At the same time, real alternatives to detached single-family suburban homes must be provided. The increased attraction of apartments near public transport, and access to projects in intermediary spaces with the potential of densification and quality of life are appropriate means of moving towards that goal. In view of the extent of already existent villa quarters, the development potential of suburban areas with respect to greater sustainability must be exploited. This as yet hardly researched field above all integrates

[34] Kurt Infanger: Les réserves de zones à bâtir sont surdimensionnées et mal situées. In: Forum du développement territorial, 2/2008. p. 39–40

considerations of densifying plots, changing existing buildings, reducing individual automotive transport and creating new services in the neighbourhood.[35]

Modular apartments – Swisswoodhouse
The project Swisswoodhouse is at the intersection between several of those themes. Its development is connected to aspects of demographic developments, urban densification and an appropriate size for residential buildings. The approach lies in developing an alternative to free-standing single-family homes in an urban or suburban environment, using local timber as a native resource.[36]
Swisswoodhouse is intended as an answer to the abovementioned problems, by applying a flexible modular building method for an apartment building. The concept plans a three-to-four storey building with two or three apartments per floor. The size is calculated to encourage neighbours to meet and thereby prevent the risk of anonymity, which is widespread in large residential complexes. The apartments are designed on the principle of a basic 22 m^2 timber module and allows users to model their future apartment as they wish, from modest to very spacious.

[35] Emmanuel Rey: Quartiers de villas, friches du futur? In: Tracés, 7/2009. p. 7–8
[36] Willi Frei / Emmanuel Rey: Architecture et développement durable: sur la piste du bois. Actes des Journées européennes de la construction en bois, Ecole nationale supérieure des technologies et industries du bois. Epinal, October 2000. p. 127–135

Each basic module can be used for a wide range of functions: an individual kitchen or kitchen with storage space, an individual room or one with a toilet, or two combined modules as a bedroom for parents with a bathroom and storage space, a room with a loggia, balcony or an entirely open terrace etc. A veritable catalogue of possible combinations has gradually developed. Modules can be combined to create studios, apartments with one to four rooms, and even penthouse apartments with up to ten modules.[37]

Such a great variety of typologies gives clients a wide range of options for possible adaptations. A system of balconies was also developed that can be attached to the façades at the end. The staircases and elevators can also be fitted into our module. They are prefabricated depending on requirements, placed on a concrete skeleton and successively connected to each other. The research project was launched together with the company Renggli and developed in cooperation with numerous partners. Diverse volumetrics and different façade cladding have been tested. Bauart did not regard wood to be essential as the building material, but the choice was the result of comprehensive considerations – especially in view of the desire for an architectural appearance that suited the relevant context. In the field of energy, a combination of measures was achieved during the research phase, thereby already fulfilling the 2000 Watt society guidelines.[38]

---

[37] Sonja Lüthi: Prototyp Swisswoodhouse. In: Viso Architektur, 4/2008. p. 76–81
[38] Vincent Borcard: La construction du futur. In: Habitation, 3/2013. p. 18–19

Following the research phase, the project began its experimental phase with the construction of an initial prototype in the Lucerne district of Nebikon. The aim is the densification of a plot that has good access to public transport services and leads to a waterway. A building with three storeys and a loft was considered there. It comprises 16 apartments with different typologies.

Basically, the question of adapting the free-standing house to social requirements is not really new. Le Corbusier already described the single-family home as a "demagogic illusion" in the 1950s, as he developed his ideas of *Unités d'habitation*.[39] With respect to the sustainable city, it is important to constantly investigate the question and prepare solutions with concrete experiments.

[39] Willy Boesiger (Ed.): Le Corbusier et son atelier rue de Sèvres 35. Œuvre complète 1957–1965. Basel/Boston/Berlin: Birkhäuser 2006 (8ème édition). p. 204–207

Swisswoodhouse

Development 2008–2012 / Construction 2013–2014
Architect: Bauart / W. Frei, R. Graf, S. Graf, P. C. Jakob,
E. Rey, Y. Ringeisen, M. Ryter
Collaboration: C. Arcayo, B. Gygax, M. Huber, F. Mani,
A. Matti, T. Meury, R. Moser, T. Nadarajah, L. Ruchet,
B. Ryf, J. Schibig, C. Seidler, S. Spiess, L. Stämpfli,
N. Trachsel-Gerber
General Contractor: Renggli AG, Reuss Engineering,
Makiol + Wiederkehr, Pirmin Jung
Academic Partners: IBB (ETH Zurich), EMPA Dübendorf,
BFH-AHB Biel, HEIG-VD Yverdon-les-Bains
Support: OFEN, OFEV, CTI

Fig. 1: Insertion into the urban environment
Fig. 2: Diversity of the modules
Fig. 3: Insertion into the suburban environment

Fig. 1

Fig. 2

Fig. 3

Reconsidering Existing Role Models

Questioning standard practice
Standard building practice entails a certain conservatism
in terms of repeating so-called tried and trusted solutions.
In doing so, one runs the risk of applying programmatic,
typological, structural and technical solutions that cannot
fulfil the demands of constantly transforming tasks.
From the perspective of sustainability – which implies taking
long term perspectives into account in decision making
processes – a critical approach that is based on research
and questioning should be developed to prevent decisions
along the lines of "building as usual".[40]
Developing alternatives requires us to question certain
established guiding principles on several levels: from spatial planning to structural details. One of the operative
difficulties lies in achieving that without costs spiralling
disproportionally.

---

[40] Emmanuel Rey: Intégration des critères de durabilité dans les straté-
gies de régénération urbaine. Conférence à l'École des Ponts ParisTech.
Champs-sur-Marne, 6 February 2013

Marin Centre

The way that principles of sustainability were taken into account in implementing the Marin Centre shopping centre – a space that is strongly determined by functional and logistic requirements – is a typical example. The planning required careful prior analysis of the location's characteristics. The replacement development distinguished itself from its predecessor through its strategic positioning at the gateway to greater Neuchâtel. Its form is influenced by the geometry of the location: It expresses the constitutive differences in the scale of the local environment.[41]

Towards the north, the shopping centre presents itself with a straight-lined façade that accommodates the multi-storey car park and picks up on the linearity of the nearby motorway. Accesses to the motorway are provided via an extremely concentrated area. All required delivery facilities are accommodated on the eastern and southern sides, whereby traffic flows can be precisely organised in a separate way. On the western side, the space of the old parking area was used to create a large public park that mediates between the scales of the motorway landscape and the neighbouring village. Rubble from the demolition of the old shopping centre was used to create a series of green pyramids that anchor the shopping centre into its context. In this way, attractive accessing routes were created for

---

[41] Christophe Catsaros: Identité urbaine et subtiles perspectives. In: Tec21/Tracés, Dossier 11/2011. p. 6–13

visitors who reach the centre on foot or by bicycle, bus or train. The staggered implementation was also tailored in a way to ensure that no interruption in retailing operations was necessary and only one moving date had to be announced.

The architecture of the building outwardly presents itself as a shell that unites the expression of the different sides. It consists of 6,400 shiny, black metal plates and 900 pixel-shaped, scattered openings. Large openings created by placing diagonal levels together produce perspectives that precisely refer to the entrances, thereby guiding visitors into the centre. Especially short distances connect the car park and the pedestrian walkway to a large central area in full sunlight, recalling an urban square.[42]

The roof of this central space is perforated by irregular openings that are sometimes big enough to see the sky and sometimes slimmer, creating an altering play of light during the course of the day and in different seasons. That space, to which all shops are directly connected, forms the heart of the shopping centre. Its simple geometric form communicates a certain permanence in the face of the changeability that is characteristic of the interior decoration of individual stores. Its shell is based on prefabricated timber construction and includes various openings to control the space's climate.[43]

[42] The new Marin Centre, Marin-Epagnier, a new shopping centre in Switzerland. In: architecturetoday.co.uk, February 2012
[43] Christophe Catsaros/Anna Hohler: Diagonales surprenantes, espaces lumineux. In: Tec21/Tracés, Dossier 11/2011. p. 22–35

The theme of energy consumption was a major part of planning to make significant reductions to the heating and power requirements. The Minergie-certified new Marin Centre has a very low consumption per m^2: approximately 20 % of the average consumption of buildings used in a comparable way in Switzerland. Compared to the previous building, the heating consumption per m^2 was reduced to a third and power requirements were reduced by half.[44]

The measures to reduce the heating requirements above all affect the thermal quality of the shell and the heat recovery of all cooling equipment. In terms of power consumption, the central space, the use of natural lighting and passive air-conditioning were the focuses, as well as the integration of active panels and a selection of especially high performance devices that use LED technology for certain applications.

In parallel to the measures in the field of energy, other environmental aspects were integrated from the start, for instance minimising exhaust emissions on the estate, an eco-friendly approach to rain water (through seepage and retention facilities), the selection of materials with a strong environmental balance-sheet (e.g. the timber construction for the roof of the central space) and a considerable increase in the species diversity on the grounds (due to green roofs and expansive meadows instead of the old car park).

---

[44] Emmanuel Rey et al.: Architecture durable en pratique. In: Tec21/ Tracés, Dossier 11/2011. p. 36–49

A supplementary photovoltaic system with solar cells was installed over an area of 6,810 m^2 of the multi-storey car park. It will contribute to increasing the proportion of renewable energy in the regional power grid.

Fig. 1

Marin Centre, La Tène

Competition 2005 / Construction period
2008–2011
Client: Marin Centre SA
Architect: Bauart / W. Frei, R. Graf, S. Graf,
P. C. Jakob, E. Rey, Y. Ringeisen, M. Ryter
Collaboration: F. Agustoni, A. Baertschi,
F. Brand, M. Bratschi, A. Bulani, M. Di Leone,
S. Fries, C. Gander, K. Gerber, Ch. Goldschmid,
Ch. Höfler, C. Hitschke, B. Jaja, Y, Jolliet,
D. Jost, O. Lehmann, D. Leuba, N. Licordari,
J. Luginbühl, R. Papisch, D. Perez, Y. Pfeiffer,
P. Remund, J. Sinatra, Th. Schmid B. Sulger-
Schleich, M. Ulmer, H. Versteeg, A. Wavre,
P. Willich, C. Zumwald
Site engineer: Atelier d'architecture
Dominique Rosset SA

Fig. 1: Central space
Fig. 2: Site plan
Fig. 3: Longitudinal section
Fig. 4: Upper level floor plan
Fig. 5: Landscape gardening

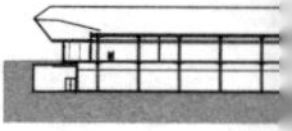

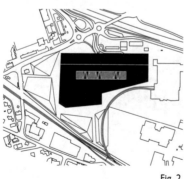

Fig. 2

Fig. 3

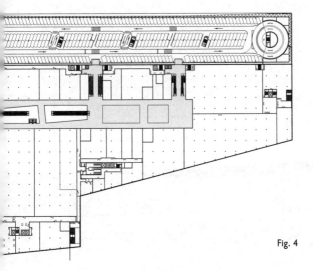

Fig. 4

Fig. 5

Integrating Technological Innovation

An undogmatic approach to technology

The construction industry is constantly developing new products. In that respect it is on the one hand a source of elements that are potentially exciting for the development of architectural approaches. On the other hand they can be a hindrance when they are inappropriate products or products with a short life cycle.

In the decades directly after the first oil crisis, ecological architecture was for a long time determined by the strong contradiction between two clearly contrasting approaches: Representatives of low-tech naturally saw the solution in refraining from all such technology. High-tech supporters believed in the intensive use of technologies aimed at solving all energy and environmental problems.[45]

A few decades later, that opposition has largely lost its sharpness, becoming more differentiated and less dogmatic. Going beyond a system of a systematic rejection or blind faith in technology, such further consideration has paved the way for new possibilities: Now measures are combined to develop strategies that are the most efficient and suitable for the relevant situation.

[45] Emmanuel Rey: Mythes et réalités de l'architecture durable. Cours «Architecture et durabilité: approches critiques», Programme doctoral «Architecture et sciences de la ville», EPFL. Lausanne, September 2013

The results are new and exciting mixtures in the field of energy. Very simple means that are in harmony with the principles of bioclimatic architecture are combined with state of the art technology in the field of renewable energies. On another level, the combination of different materials enables a reduction in the consumption of grey energy and the volume of the material used, by using the advantages of each individual element.

Microcity
The construction of a research centre for microtechnology in the heart of the city of Neuchâtel provided the opportunity for several hybrid measures in the field of spatial planning, technology and construction.

On a spatial level, the building is integrated as a significant pole in the urban morphology. Beginning with a regular interior grid of 7.20 x 7.20 metres, its sculptural design reacts to the special characteristics of the immediate surroundings. That results in a structuring of the location, not only in the case of the spaces of the building's interior, but also in terms of the public exterior facilities. Due to the exchange with the new part of the city, the existing buildings and the exterior spaces create a new identity and coherence that enhances the entire quarter.

The interplay with the compact nature of the proposed building and the creation of new exterior spaces allows the topography of the terrain to accommodate a dialogue that is "tailored" for the location. The park with exclusively native plant species and a retention basin for rainwater creates connections with the neighbouring quarter and turns it into a prestigious area of the new campus. The wall of cliffs to the north is also comprehensively greened to create a rich contrast between the green areas and the building.

The building, which is conceived as a small city, expresses itself as a spatial continuum that is determined by a rich, tight-meshed network of the main distribution routes, auxiliary pathways and zones in which to linger. This concept results in a series of open platforms that facilitate the spontaneous exchange between users. The common areas, especially the auditorium, the foyer and cafeteria, are connected to the central axis at the heart of the building. It structures access to the building and forms a spatial reference that connects the entrances, leads along the interior thoroughfares and integrates the large stairs. The construction initially consists of three concrete cores that accommodate the technology required for the functions of the building.

Furthermore the construction is based on a hybrid system of wood and concrete that allows a reduction of grey energy, an increased level of flexibility and many opportunities for later adaptation.[46]

The clear distribution of proposed systems is not only based on a conceptual, functional and technical approach, but is also aimed at the efficiency of the project – both on an economic level (optimising the construction and utilization costs) and on an operative level. The prefabrication

---

[46] Emilie Veillon: Microcity: un projet hybride en bois-béton. In: Batimag, 1/2012. p. 6–10

of a large part of the construction in the workshop aided fast construction work and reduced any inconvenience to the neighbourhood due to work on the building site.

Using the special characteristics of the programme and the building site, the project takes ecological, socio-cultural and economic criteria into account. The procedure is based on solutions that mainly focus on a rational resource budget (land, energy, water, species diversity) and minimising environmental burdens (sustainable mobility, compact building, thermal quality of the building shell, materials with a good environmental balance sheet).

Microcity is also a driving force for integrating renewable energies going beyond its own limits: on the one hand by installing a photovoltaic centre on the roof that is connected to the city's power grid, and one the other by creating an underground canal ring that uses water from the lake to air-condition several buildings in the quarter.

Fig. 1

Microcity, Neuchâtel

Competition 2010 (in cooperation with
ERNE Holzbau AG)/Construction period
2010–2014
Client: Canton of Neuchâtel
User: École Polytechnique Fédérale de
Lausanne (EPFL)
General Contractor: ERNE Holzbau AG
Architect: Bauart/W. Frei, R. Graf, S. Graf,
P. C. Jakob, E. Rey, Y. Ringeisen, M. Ryter
Collaboration: F. Couture, G. Detruche,
L. Di Prinzio, F. Imthon-Zweifel, Y. Jolliet,
O. Lehmann, E. Shehi, R. Sulzer, M. Ulmer,
A. Wavre, V. Wörner

Fig. 1: Insertion into the city
Fig. 2: Site plan
Fig. 3: Constructive principle
Fig. 4: Assembly of the hybrid elements

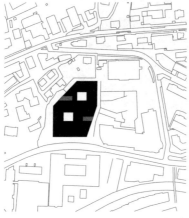

Fig. 2

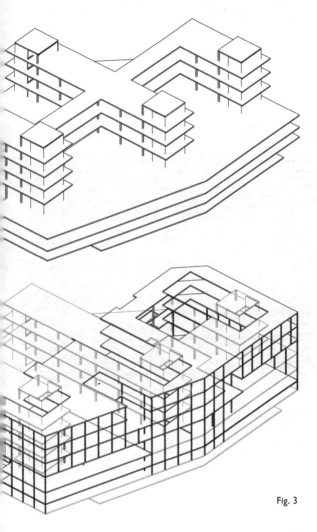

Fig. 3

Fig. 4

For a Creative Approach to Sustainability

The search for an ever better balance between ecological, socio-cultural and economic criteria is an integral element of every sustainable architectural project. On a conceptual level, the principle of optimisation may be easy to develop, but it is especially important that its implementation requires continued supervision and coordination between the various dimensions of the project.

Generally, these different dimensions cannot be achieved equally on the highest level. All project participants – be it on the level of spatial planning or on an urban or architectural level – must be willing to strive towards optimisation in their approach, which involves a process of weighing up different interests to achieve the best results with respect to the overall parameters considered. That approach is not limited to merely recording results, but insists on the importance of the approach taken and on adhering to it during the entire construction process. In that sense it is necessary to always make decisions based on a full awareness of all the facts.

In recognition of this operative complexity, we concur in this respect with François Ascher that, "sustainable development cannot produce stone tablets or make commandments for all to follow one plan." Instead, it constitutes a problem that, "determines the main questions to be considered in analyses and decisions, and of which decision-makers must remain aware."[47] From that perspective, integrating the factor of sustainability in architecture can enrich the procedure of a project, although it does not involve any fewer considerations. Nevertheless, it can lead to long-term and above all more explicit decisions.

The complexity of transformation processes in urban regions requires the search for innovative solutions, during both the design and construction phases, and also with respect to the buildings' use. In this context, strategies must be found to reclaim the urban space. The aim is not only to achieve sensible levels of resource consumption, but also to create the basis for a new attraction to cities and conurbations. The architectural project plays a central role in this multifaceted task. Its integrative character indeed makes it a means by which to investigate spatial, typological and technical alternatives that encourage development towards a sustainable constructed environment.

Striving towards the sustainability of the developed environment through the architectural project means implicitly recognising the significance of creativity in these evolutionary processes. In view of the large number of parameters that must be integrated, it indeed appears to be fundamental that the participants can support the pioneering role of the project with a certain degree of inventiveness on the level of processes that are connected to the production of a quality building.

[47] François Ascher: La République contre la ville. Essai sur l'avenir de la France urbaine. La Tour d'Aigues: Ed. De l'Aube 1998

On condition of receiving essential compensation for the additional performance provided, the architect can pool the available driving forces, find undogmatic mechanisms to overcome any obstacles and structure the process of exchange between the different units involved. Alternating between the roles of "creator", "developer" and "mediator", he assumes a key role for the success of the project. That requires not only competences in the actual field of design and project implementation, but also certainly the ability to surround oneself with parameters that are ideally suited to the relevant purpose.[48]

In fact this meeting between different – both creative and pragmatic – converging intentions is an opportunity to turn sustainability in architecture into a concrete entity.[49] We should note that the critical observation of implemented projects is also decisive. The aim is to continuously learn from the implementation of ground-breaking projects and thereby combine the dynamism required for any pioneering performance with the continuity of a perspective that focuses on the long term. Processes will always develop from this spirit of innovation, investigation and optimisation that can truly drive forward a "sustainable development, now more than ever."[50]

[48] Emmanuel Rey: Quels processus pour la création d'un quartier durable: l'exemple du projet Ecoparc à Neuchâtel. In: Urbia, 4/2007 p. 123–145
[49] Benedikt Loderer: The state of the Bauart. In: Heinz Wirz et al.: Bauart. Lucerne: Quart Verlag 2008. p. 8–13
[50] Antonio Da Cunha / Jean Ruegg: Pour un développement durable en train de se faire. In: Ibid.: Développement durable et aménagement du territoire. Lausanne: PPUR 2003. p. 347–350

The Author and the Office

Emmanuel Rey

After graduating in Architecture at the EPFL Lausanne (1997), Emmanuel Rey achieved a post-graduate degree in Architecture and Sustainable Development (1999) in parallel with his work, before achieving his doctorate at the Université Catholique de Louvain (UCL, 2006), for which he was awarded the Prix européen Gustave Magnel in 2009. As a partner in the office Bauart Architects and Planners Ltd in Bern, Neuchâtel and Zurich, he has participated in numerous projects that have been published and exhibited in diverse contexts, as well as winning awards.

Since 2010 he has also been Professor at the Institute of Architecture and the City (IA) in the School for Architecture, Civil and Environmental Engineering (ENAC) of the École Polytechnique Fédérale de Lausanne (EPFL), where he has developed the Laboratory of Architecture and Sustainable Technologies (LAST). His focus lies in research and teaching in the field of sustainable architecture, especially implementing principles of sustainability on various levels of measures – from urban development projects down to individual elements of building – as well as the integration of innovative evaluation criteria into the architectural project.

last.epfl.ch

Bauart

The office Bauart Architects and Planners Ltd is based in Bern, Neuchâtel and Zurich and was founded in 1987. Today it has around 60 employees, including almost 40 architects. Willi Frei, Raffael Graf, Stefan Graf, Peter C. Jakob, Emmanuel Rey, Yorick Ringeisen and Marco Ryter are the seven partners of the office.

The activities of Bauart cover many fields of architecture and urban development. The office is dedicated both to new buildings and converting existing structures. It is characterised by the initiation, development, supervision and implementation of creative, innovative and ambitious ideas. Achieving sustainable solutions that significantly contribute to improving the quality of the developed environment forms a special focus of operations. The office's partners are also represented in various expert associations such as the Federation of Swiss Architects (FAS), the Swiss Society of Engineers and Architects (SIA), the Federation of Swiss Planners (FSU), the Schweizer Werkbund (SWB), Swissolar, Cobaty international and the Association Ecoparc.

www.bauart.ch

Acknowledgements

The publication of this book would not have been possible without the support of numerous people, whom I warmly thank. Special thanks to:

Jean-Paul Felley and Olivier Kaeser, the Directors of the Centre culturel suisse de Paris, for supporting this project,

Willi Frei, Raffael Graf, Stefan Graf, Peter C. Jakob, Yorick Ringeisen and Marco Ryter, my management partners in the Bauart office in Bern, Neuchâtel und Zurich, as well as our employees, for their constant input,

All participants in the various projects presented in this volume, especially representatives of the cantonal and municipal administrations, members of public service providers, property owners, clients, engineers, specialists, building contractors and users,

Pro Helvetia, the Swiss Arts Council, whose support has made it possible to publish this book in several languages,

Heinz Wirz of the Quart publishing house in Lucerne, for his professional and committed supervision of the publication,

Sophie Lufkin, Senior Scientist at the Laboratory of Architecture and Sustainable Technologies of the EPFL, for her critical and attentive reading of the texts,

Ariane Wavre, responsible for PR at Bauart, for her support in coordinating and proofreading the work,

my family and friends who have made a significant contribution to the success of this publication through their direct or indirect support.

Quart Publishers Lucerne

Notatio – Short texts on architecture and art

1 Ignasi de Solà-Morales: Mediations in Architecture
  and in the Urban Landscape (de and en)
2 Bart Verschaffel: Architecture is (as) a gesture
  (de and en)
3 Stadtlicht. Ein Farb-Licht-Projekt für Basel (de)
4 Emmanuel Rey: From Spatial Development to Detail
  (de, en and fr)

Bibliotheca – Writings on architecture and art

1 Francesco Collotti: Architekturtheoretische Notizen
  (de and it)
2 Markus Breitschmid: Der bauende Geist (de)
3 Miroslav Šik: Altneue Gedanken (de)
4 Manfred Sack: Verlockungen der Architektur (de)

Quart Verlag GmbH, Heinz Wirz, Denkmalstrasse 2,
CH-6006 Luzern; books@quart.ch, www.quart.ch